magic lanterns

MAGIC LANTERNS was inspired by the wonderful
Glasgow Lantern Procession organized by Welfare
State International Theatre Company. The book
is dedicated to all those involved in the South
Devon Steiner School, which is a constant source
of inspiration.

First published in North America in 2002 by
North Light Books
an imprint of F&W Publications, Inc.
4700 East Galbraith Road
Cincinnati, OH 45236
1-800/289-0963

Library of Congress Cataloguing-in-Publication
Data is available

ISBN: 1-58180-248-X

Senior Editor: **Clare Churly**
Editor: **Michelle Pickering**
Designer: **Georgina Rhodes**
Photographer: **Peter Williams**

Color reproduction by Global Colour, Malaysia
Printed by Craft Print International Ltd

Safety information is provided on pages 10–11.
The author, publisher and copyright owner accept
no responsibility for any damage or injury caused
or sustained while using the products, techniques
or finished projects outlined in this book.

Creative projects for making and decorating lanterns for indoors and out

magic lanterns

Mary Maguire

Photographs Peter Williams

NORTH LIGHT BOOKS
Cincinnati, Ohio

Contents

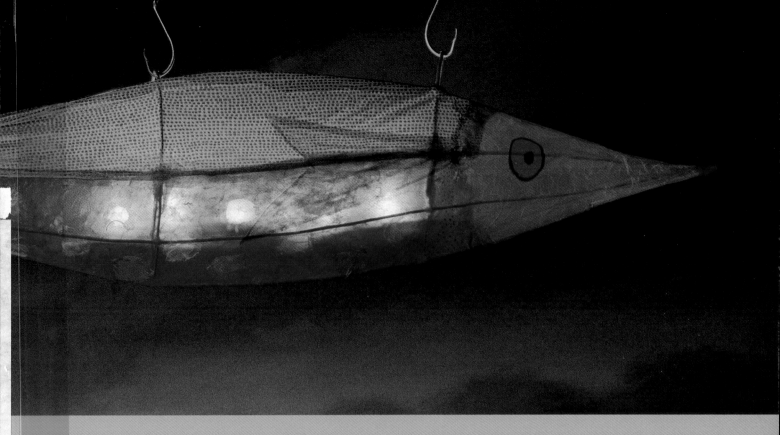

Introduction

In the days before gas and electricity the main sources of artificial light were oil lamps and candles. A lantern around the flame prevented it from being extinguished while offering some protection to the home from fire. It wasn't long before candle-light was being enhanced by surrounding it with a lantern that added color and form to the basic light source, turning it into something wondrous. We no longer have a practical need for lanterns, but emotionally they fulfill a need— a yearning for simplicity. They cast a warm and nurturing light that is soothing in our busy, stress-filled lives.

Lantern processions have long been popular in parts of Europe, with whole communities taking part. Now they are happening in the United States and United Kingdom, too. The range of lanterns varies widely from the simple painted glass jar suspended on a string, to bent-willow structures covered in painted tissue paper and huge, illuminated bamboo, wire, and fabric carnival floats. Children can carry lanterns illuminated by a small flashlight or bicycle light on a stick. These processions can celebrate a local or national event, the changing seasons, an anniversary or they can highlight a good cause.

In the home, lanterns can be used to create ambient lighting for special occasions, Halloween or Christmas, and for safety light bulbs can be used in these lanterns. Outdoor lanterns look enchanting hung from a tree, lining a pathway, or floating on a pond for a magical garden party.

Whatever your interest in lanterns, you will find achievable projects in this book, which contains detailed step-by-step instructions and inspiring photographs of the finished article. Happy lantern making!

Materials and Equipment

The following items are widely used in the projects in this book. Wire cutters, jewelry pliers, pruning shears, and tapes are necessary for creating many of the structures. An assortment of translucent papers, colored pens, paints, and inks will be useful for decorating and adorning the lanterns.

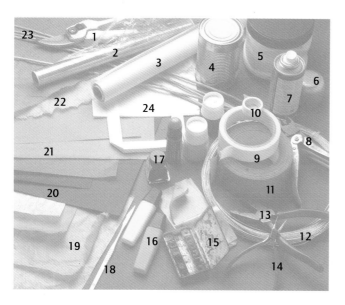

1 Pruning shears (secateurs)	13 Household pliers
2 Plastic wrap (clingfilm)	14 Jewelry pliers
3 Oil-resistant baking paper	15 Watercolor paints
4 Empty food cans	16 Felt tip pens
5 Paste mixture (see p.14)	17 Watercolor inks
6 Glass paints	18 Fine-bladed craft knife
7 Frosting spray	19 Silk tissue paper
8 Wire cutters	20 Thick cardstock
9 Masking tape	21 Ordinary tissue paper
10 Surgical tape	22 Handmade paper
11 Heavy-duty tape	23 Willow sticks (withies)
12 Galvanized wire	24 Paper bag

Safety and Illumination

Extreme care must be taken with lanterns that are lit by candles. Make sure that you never leave lit candles unattended and always supervise children with them. Here are some useful tips on safety and alternative ways to light lanterns, including electrical and chemical lights. Think carefully about how your lantern will be used and choose the best method of illumination accordingly. For example, the large moon lantern (see p.88) needs one flashlight pointing down from the top, one pointing up from the bottom, and one pointing forward from the center back to illuminate the face.

1 Candles in glass jars: Tea lights are the safest type of candle to use. Put a double-sided adhesive mounting pad on the base of the light and stick it centrally to the base of a glass jar. This will stop the tea light from moving and creating hot spots on the glass. If you wish to use an ordinary small candle, fix it in the same way and surround it with a layer of sand. An old food jar can be used for most projects, but a finer glass container, such as the one shown here, may be necessary for very lightweight structures. If you use this type of container, make sure that the sides are not too close to the paper surface of the lantern.

2 Other containers: Tea lights or small candles can be placed inside clean, empty food cans. These can then be attached to wire mesh cages and suspended or supported within the structure of a lantern. Foil containers can be used in the same way.

3 Flame-retardant coating: This can be purchased from theatrical suppliers and painted directly onto fabric or paper without altering the appearance. It is important to remember that this is only a retardant, however, and it does not make the material fireproof.

4 Lantern handles: If you are making a lantern with a handle, make sure that the handle is long enough for you to carry the lantern comfortably without your hand getting too hot. This is also important if you plan to hang up the lantern, so that the object from which the lantern is suspended does not catch fire. If the handle is not rigid, extinguish the flame before allowing the handle to rest over the lantern.

5 Electrical and chemical lights: If a battery-operated light is to be suspended within a structure, it must be lightweight, and the beam of light should radiate in as many directions as possible. If they are to be laid on a flat surface, choose flat-backed lights. Small key-ring lights are useful for illuminating small areas. Chemical light sticks are available in a variety of colors. Once activated, they will glow for a long time (see packaging for exact details) but cannot be switched off. They do, however, have the advantage of being very bright.

6 Christmas lights: Strings of electric lights, which are suitable for either indoor or outdoor use, can be very safe and effective. Choose lights that have low-heat bulbs and make sure that the bulbs do not touch the sides of the lanterns. Each set varies, so it is important that you comply with the manufacturer's instructions. Tiny battery-operated christmas lights, designed for use with flower arrangements, can be inserted into dried poppy heads or Chinese lantern seedpods.

Creating Structures

Most of the lanterns in this book have a framework that is made from either galvanized wire or flexible, slender, young willow twigs (withies). Galvanized wire is available in a range of thicknesses from hardware stores, and willow sticks (withies) can be bought from craft suppliers or florists. The following techniques show you how to create lantern structures with these materials.

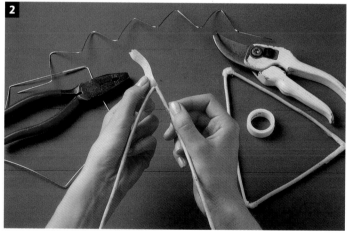

1 Bending curves: To bend wire into a smooth curve, wrap it around a former, such as a glass jar, food can, or cylindrical pipe. Secure the ends together with surgical tape to form a circle. To create a decorative scroll, hold the wire with jewelry pliers and bend it around to form a small loop. Grip the loop flat between the jaws of a pair of household pliers, then wind the wire around, keeping it taut all the while. To bend willow sticks (withies), soak them for a day, then bend them into shape, securing the ends together with surgical tape if you wish to form a circle.

2 Bending angles: To bend wire at an angle, hold it firmly with household or jewelry pliers at the appropriate position and bend sharply. Open out the angle to the required position. To bend willow sticks (withies), soak them for for a day, then make a crease at the appropriate position with your

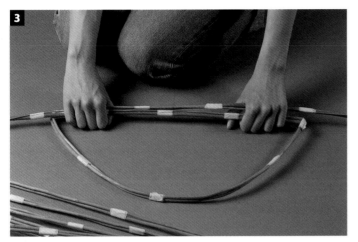

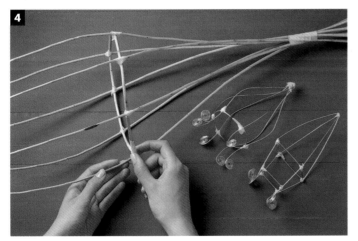

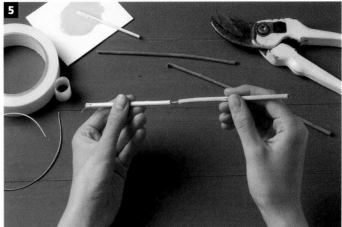

thumbnail. Hold them on either side of the crease, with the crease facing you, and bend the ends toward you. If the willow splinters at the back of the bend, cover it with surgical tape.

3 Experimenting with willow sticks (withies): When you use natural materials such as willow sticks (withies), you must accept that each stick is different, and you will never be able to achieve perfect symmetry, but they are wonderful to work with.

When making large lantern structures, single willow sticks (withies) are not strong enough, so tape them together in pairs with masking tape, thick end to thin end. This will make an even thickness.

4 Size of framework: Always bear in mind that you need to create enough of a framework onto which to attach the decorative tissue paper. Large pieces of paper that do not have sufficient support beneath them are more difficult to apply and more

likely to tear. An adequate framework is also necessary to help make sure that any paper covering is not too close to the light source.

5 Making invisible joints: Generally, willow sticks (withies) can be joined using tape. If you need to create an invisible joint, however, insert a length of fine wire down the center of the two willow sticks (withies), spread glue over the two ends, then push them together until the wire disappears.

6 Taping wire and willow sticks (withies): When taping willow sticks (withies) or wire together, make sure that they are joined securely. Surgical tape is best for small structures, masking tape for medium ones, and heavy-duty electrical tape for large ones. When taping an intersection, apply tape across both directions.

Covering Structures

When covering lantern structures you will need attractively colored paper that is strong, light, and translucent. Handmade papers, especially those with fibrous threads integral to the paper, are generally stronger and so more suitable for larger lantern structures. Some types of tissue paper fade easily, so if you are using these, then store them away from direct sunlight. The following techniques show you how to make your lanterns strong and durable.

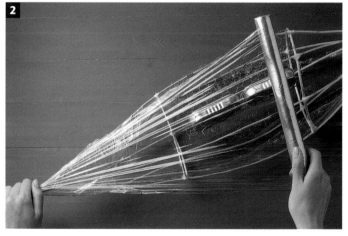

1 Making paste: A strong, effective paste for gluing paper onto lanterns can be made by mixing a 50:50 ratio of wallpaper paste and craft glue. Mix the wallpaper paste as directed in the manufacturer's instructions, then slowly add the glue, stirring all the time. The wallpaper paste makes the glue slippery, which allows you to reposition the paper if necessary.

2 Strengthening lanterns: To add durability without losing luminosity, cover your structure with plastic wrap (clingfilm), stretching it as smoothly as possible. Tissue paper can be glued on top of this, making it more robust and minimizing tears.

3 Diffusing the light: Covering a lantern with a base layer of white tissue paper before adding layers of colored paper helps to diffuse the light. This is particularly useful for large lanterns. Allow the base layer to dry thoroughly before adding the colored layers.

4 Applying tissue paper: For small lanterns, draw around the shape required, allowing extra on curved edges plus a ¹⁄₂in (1cm) overlap on all sides. Apply paste to the paper and attach it to the structure, smoothing any wrinkles. Wrap the edges around the framework. It is difficult to work in this way on a large scale because wet tissue is hard to maneuver without ripping, so work with small, randomly torn pieces of paper stuck over a plastic wrap base instead.

Do not worry if you tear or pierce a paper lantern: it is easily repaired. Just paste fresh pieces of tissue paper over the whole area. Do not simply paste paper over the tear or it will remain visible.

5 Creating patterns: Build up patterns by pasting different colored pieces of paper next to each other. Alternatively, apply a base layer of paper in one color. When dry, cut shapes from it using a craft knife, then cover the gaps with a different colored paper to create an attractive pattern.

6 Forming flaps: On large structures that are lit with battery-operated flashlights, you need access to switch the flashlights on and off and to change the batteries. Make flaps by cutting out three sides of a doorway, leaving the fourth side attached. Glue an extra ¹⁄₂in (1cm) of tissue paper all around the three cut sides and allow to dry. Stick Velcro pads on the corners of the flap and the corresponding areas on the door frame so that you can open and close the flap.

Paper Bag Lanterns

A grocery bag can be transformed into a lantern by inserting a tea light into a glass jar. Decorate the bag with colored inks and pens. A check pattern is effective and easy to do, but you can indulge in more elaborate designs and pictures if you are feeling particularly creative. At a children's party, each child could decorate his or her own bag.

Materials (for each lantern)

- White paper bag with handles
- Watercolor inks
- Water-based felt tip pens
- Sand
- Tea light
- Glass jar
- Double-sided adhesive
  mounting pad

Equipment

- Broad paintbrush
- Medium paintbrush
- Fine paintbrush

1 Paint the handles and sides of each bag using bright, vibrant watercolor inks. You may want to paint each one a different color. Use broad brushstrokes and work quickly so that the paper does not become saturated.

2 Create a check pattern on the front and back of the bag by painting vertical and horizontal stripes. For an interesting design, alternate the thickness of the brushes and the color of the inks.

3 Use water-based felt tip pens to create finer patterns or to accentuate an area or to tidy up edges. Fluorescent colors work especially well.

4 Fill the base of the bag with sand to stabilize it. Stick a tea light inside a glass jar using a double-sided adhesive mounting pad (see p.10) and embed the jar in the sand.

Frosted Jars

Glass jars make the simplest and most effective lanterns. They protect the carrier from the flame and the flame from drafts (draughts), without restricting the glow of light. The pattern on the jars is created by using paper stickers and frosting spray, both of which are available from art and craft suppliers. A length of wire threaded through clear plastic tubing, which you will find in aquarium or craft stores, makes a handle that is comfortable to carry.

Materials

(for each lantern)

- Glass jar
- Assortment of self-adhesive paper stickers
- Frosting spray
- Galvanized wire
- Plastic tubing
- Tea light
- Double-sided adhesive mounting pad

Equipment

- Scissors
- Protective gloves
- Dressmaker's pin and/or craft knife
- Cotton swabs (buds)
- Lighter fluid
- Wire cutters
- Jewelry pliers

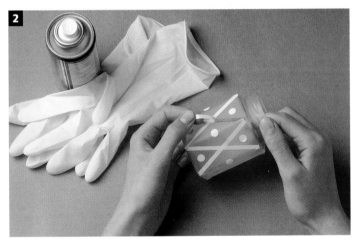

1 Create a pattern on a clean glass jar using a variety of self-adhesive paper stickers.

2 Spray the jar with frosting spray, following the instructions on the can. Do this outdoors or in a well-ventilated area, wearing gloves to protect your hands. When the frosting is dry, peel off the stickers.

3 If any of the stickers are difficult to remove, use a dressmaker's pin or craft knife to help, but be careful not to scratch any of the frosting.

Remove any adhesive left behind by the stickers with a cotton swab dipped in lighter fluid.

4 Cut a length of wire and wrap it around the neck of the jar, using jewelry pliers to form two small loops on opposite sides of the jar. Twist the ends of the wire around each other tightly to secure the wire in place. Cut a longer piece of wire, and thread it through a length of plastic tubing, allowing 1in (2.5cm) of wire to project at each end. Push these down

through the loops on the jar, then bend them upward with pliers. Squeeze these hooks tightly closed to secure the handle to the jar. Stick a tea light in the jar with a double-sided adhesive mounting pad (see p.10).

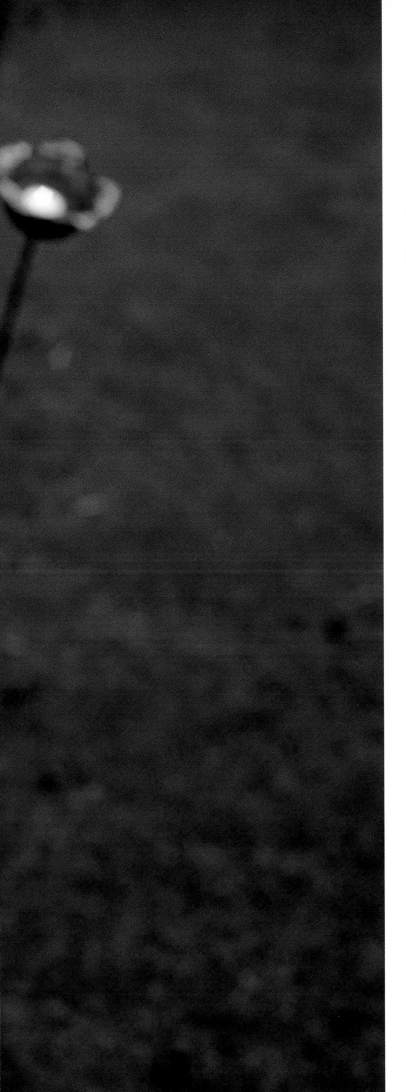

Garden Flowers

Add a touch of enchantment to a midsummer party with these fabulous flower lanterns. Made from foil containers cut into petal shapes, they are fixed onto bamboo sticks, which can be pushed into the ground. Use them to put a shimmer in your shrubbery or to illuminate a pathway, but make sure they are positioned where they will not be brushed against or accidently knocked over.

Materials (for each lantern)

- Thick felt tip pens suitable for use on metal
- 1 medium and 1 small round foil container
- Glass paints
- 1 upholstery nail with a broad, flat top and narrow shank
- Double-sided adhesive mounting pad
- Tea light
- Bamboo stick, preferably green
- Strong glue

Equipment

- Scissors
- Broad paintbrush
- Glue applicator

1 Draw a five- or six-petaled flower around the outside of a medium foil container, making sure that the petals are roughly the same size. Cut out carefully with scissors.

2 Paint the inside and outside of the flower with a thick, even coating of glass paint. Use different colors inside and out if you wish. Allow the paint to dry, then use a thick pen to delineate the edges of the petals. Paint a small foil container in a contrasting color.

3 Place the small container inside the larger flower container. Push an upholstery nail through the center so that it emerges from the inside of the containers through the base. Stick a double-sided adhesive mounting pad to the bottom of a tea light.

4 Push the protruding end of the nail into the center of a bamboo stick and apply a drop of strong glue to hold it in position. Stick the tea light in the center of the flower.

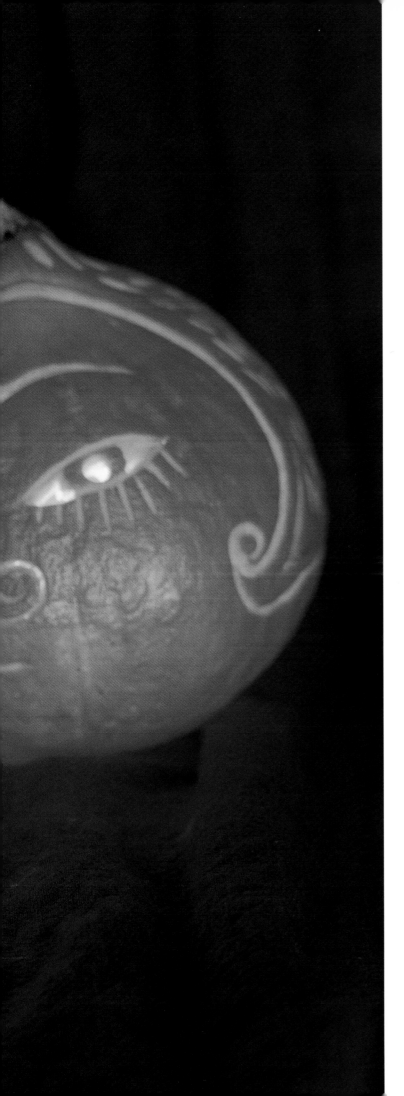

Carved Squash

With a set of carving or linoleum-cutting tools, the scope for decorating pumpkins is immense, so why not try something different from the traditional Jack-o-lantern? Remember that the deeper you carve, the better the pattern will appear. Delicate patterns can be carved just below the surface of the skin, but you will need to hollow out more of the inside for them to be visible. Remember to use a lamp or flashlight, rather than a candle, to light your lantern if you want to keep the lid on the squash while it is illuminated.

Materials

- Pumpkin or squash
- Water-based felt tip pen
- Permanent marker pen
- Cooking oil
- Tea light

Equipment

- Apple corer
- Assortment of linoleum-
  cutting tools and/or
  pumpkin- or wood-
  carving tools
- Small, thin saw
- Sharp knife
- Ice-cream scoop
  and/or large spoon
- Paper towels

1 Look at the shape of the squash or pumpkin and decide on a suitable design. Experiment with a water-based pen so that you can wash off any mistakes. When you are satisfied, draw the design with a permanent marker pen.

2 Carve the pattern on the top of the squash or pumpkin, using an apple corer to make holes and using cutting and carving tools to form grooves. Make a groove around the lid area.

3 Carve the pattern on the sides. When making flowing curves, take care that the edge of the blade does not dip below the skin or it will tear rather than create the design on the surface. For safety, always work with the blade pointing away from you and never hold the fruit with your hand in front of the blade.

4 Saw around the groove of the lid edge. Remove the lid and score the inside of the pumpkin or squash with a knife, taking care not to pierce the skin. Scoop out the flesh with an ice-cream scoop or a large spoon. Use paper towels to rub some cooking oil over the carved pattern on the outside to help stop the skin from drying out. Place a tea light inside.

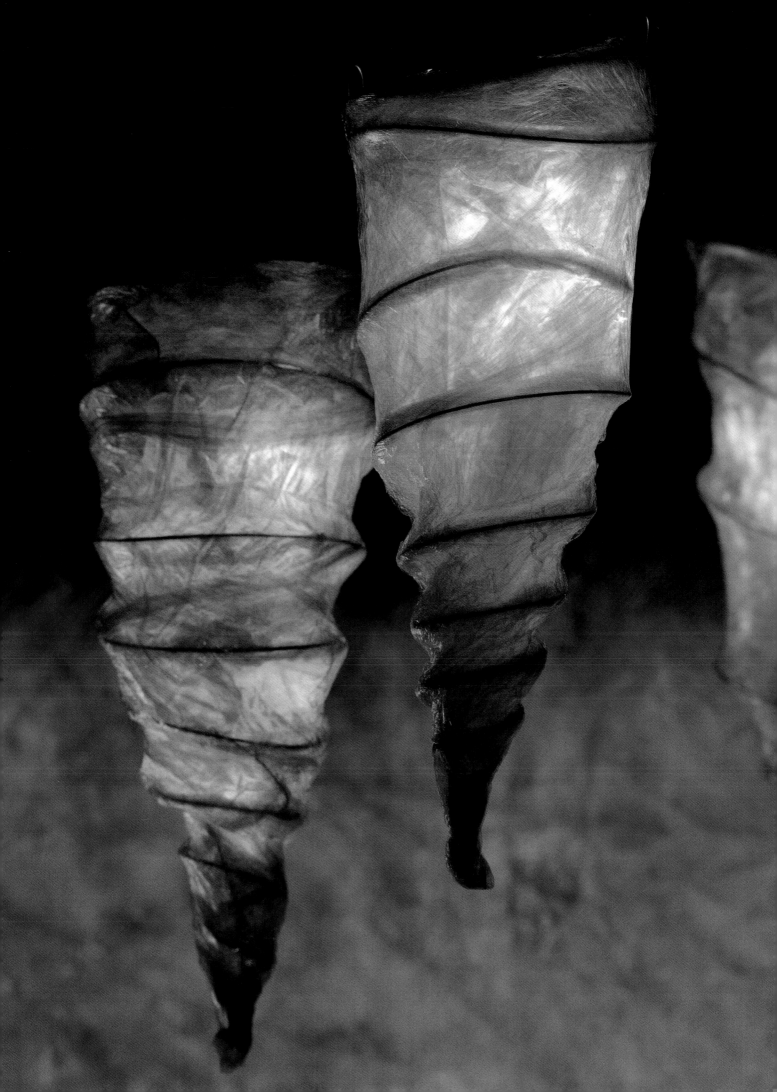

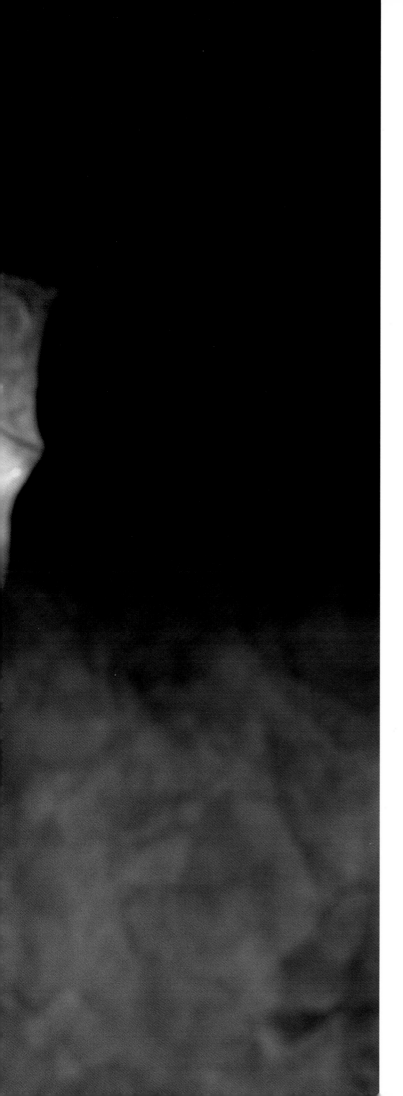

Icicles

Plastic tubing, plastic wrap, and hair nets are not the most orthodox of craft materials, but they marry together to make these mysterious chrysalis-like icicles. Iridescent cellophane adds a touch of Jack Frost's magic. Reflective bicycle lights are suspended on hair nets within the icicles, allowing the light to be directed down to the tips.

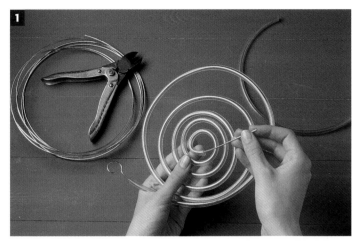

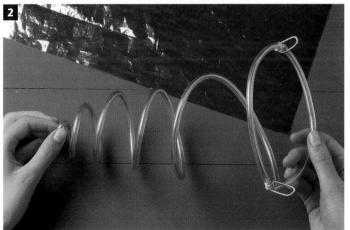

Materials (for each lantern)

- 5ft (150cm) galvanized wire
- 5ft (150cm) plastic tubing
- Iridescent cellophane
- White hair net
- Plastic wrap (clingfilm)
- White bicycle light

Equipment

- Wire cutters
- Tape measure
- Household pliers
- Scissors

1 Thread the galvanized wire through the plastic tubing, allowing approximately 2in (5cm) of wire to protrude at each end. Wind the wire into a spiral shape. The circumference of the outermost spiral should be 5–8in (12–20cm).

2 Wrap the end of the outermost wire around the nearest spiral to form a circle. Use pliers to bend the wire end into a large loop (see p.12). Cut a small length of wire to form a matching loop at the opposite side of the circle. Pull the center of the spiral downward to make a cone shape.

3 Crumple some cellophane and push it down into the center of the cone. Stretch the hair net over the rim of the top circle of wire.

4 Wind plastic wrap (clingfilm) around the structure until you get an icicle-like effect, adding shredded cellophane between the layers. When finished, push the center of the hair net down into the body of the icicle and suspend the bicycle light inside it.

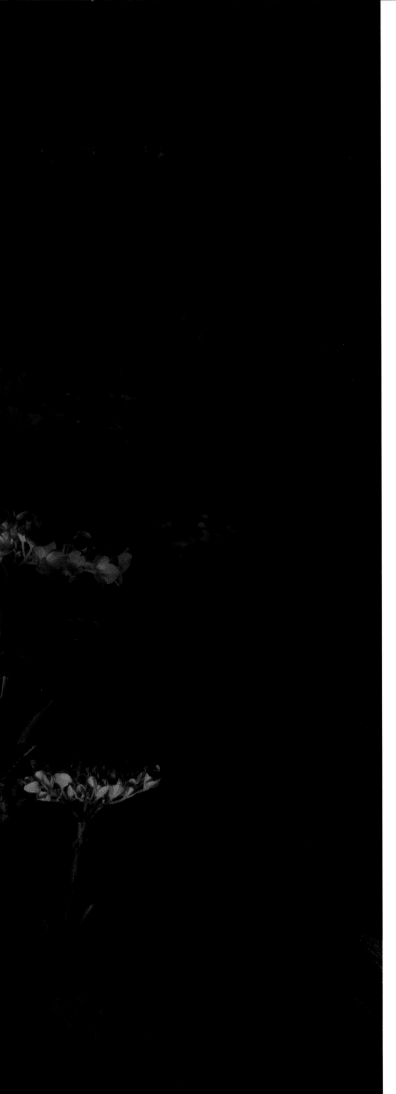

Chinese Lanterns

Chinese lanterns, made from charming floral fabric, can be hung from trees or bushes for a summer party. The fabric is stiffened with interfacing and the lantern is illuminated from within by tea lights inside glass jars. Choose tall, slim jars for an elegant shape, but make sure that the candles are fixed centrally inside the jars so that hot spots do not develop on the glass. Use a taper to light them.

Materials

(for each lantern)

- Floral fabric
- Glass jar
- Medium or heavyweight iron-on transfer paper (interfacing)
- 1in (2.5cm) wide strong double-sided adhesive tape
- Galvanized wire
- 3 brass cotter pins (split pins)
- 3 silver grommets (split-pin disks)
- Tea light
- Double-sided adhesive mounting pad

Equipment

- Scissors
- Ruler
- Iron
- Pencil
- Eyelet punch
- Wire cutters
- Jewelry pliers

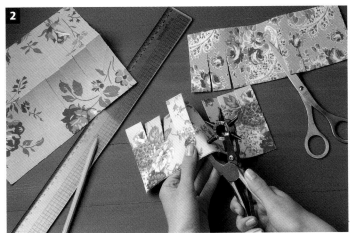

1 Cut a rectangle of fabric wide enough to wrap around the glass jar with a 1in (2.5cm) overlap and approximately 1½in (4cm) deeper than the jar. For the handle you will need a strip of fabric 1in (2.5cm) wide with a length equal to approximately four times the height of the jar (see p.11). Apply iron-on transfer paper (interfacing) to both pieces.

2 Fold the fabric in half along its length, wrong sides together, and iron flat. Draw a faint line along the length of the fabric 1½in (4cm) from the cut edge. Mark 1in (2.5cm) intervals along this line and along the folded edge of the fabric. Cut from the fold to each corresponding point on the marked line. Punch three holes ½in (1.25cm) in from the unfolded edge, positioning one hole ½in (1.25cm) from each side and another in the center.

3 Use strong double-sided adhesive tape to stick the ends of the fabric handle together to form a loop. Stand the glass jar inside the loop on the joint. Cut a length of wire and wrap it around the neck of the jar, trapping the fabric handle inside the wire. Use pliers to twist the ends of the wire together tightly so that the handle cannot move about.

4 Punch a hole in the center of the fabric on each side of the handle just above the wire. Open out the fringed piece of fabric and wrap it around the jar. Slide a brass cotter pin (split pin) through a silver grommet (split-pin disk), and then through the corresponding holes on the fringed fabric and the handle on both sides of the jar. Insert a pin and disk through the punched holes in the base of the fringed fabric. Hold the base of the fabric in line with the bottom of the jar with pieces of adhesive tape. Stick a tea light inside the jar with a double-sided adhesive mounting pad (see p.10).

Goblin Night Light

This five-sided lantern provides a warm sunset glow through the silhouettes of frolicking fairies (a template is provided). Light it in a child's room at night while reading a bedtime story, but never leave it lit when the child is unattended. Always remove the glass jar and tea light before picking up the lantern because it is not designed to be carried.

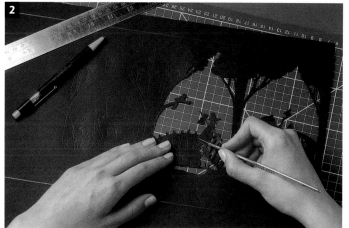

Materials

- Thick black cardstock
- Sticky tack (Blu-Tack)
- Masking tape
- Oil-resistant (greaseproof) baking paper
- Yellow, orange, pink, purple, and blue watercolor inks
- Craft glue
- Tea light
- Glass jar
- Double-sided adhesive mounting pad

Equipment

- Fine-bladed craft knife
- Ruler
- Cutting board
- Ballpoint pen
- Photocopy of stencil (see p.94)
- Dressmaker's pin
- Broad paintbrush
- Iron
- Brush and bowl for glue
- Wooden tongue depresssor or similar implement

1 Cut a 20 x 12in (50.75 x 30.5cm) rectangle of black cardstock and leave it on the cutting board. Draw a ³⁄₄in (2cm) deep margin along the top long edge and a 2³⁄₄in (7cm) one along the bottom. Fix the stencil between these two borders with sticky tack (Blu-Tack). Trace around the picture, pressing firmly, with a ballpoint pen.

2 Use a fine-bladed craft knife to cut around the silhouette. Cut out the fine details first because this is harder to do when a lot of the background has been removed. For example, cut out the spaces between the railings on the bridge before the rest of the background.

3 Pierce an eye in each figure with a dressmaker's pin. Then cut out fifteen star shapes along the top border, evenly spacing three stars between each tree trunk. If you make any mistakes, simply reposition the cut piece of cardstock and stick it in place with masking

tape at the back, then recut along the correct lines.

4 With the ruler and craft knife, score along the top and bottom margins, then score vertical lines through the center of the trees. Take care not to press the knife too hard and cut through the cardstock (again, mistakes can be rectified with masking tape). Cut slits in the cardstock from the top and bottom margins out to the edges of the card at 4in (10cm) intervals.

5 Cut a strip of oil-resistant (greaseproof) baking paper that will cover all of the black cardstock except the bottom margin. Paint bands of color across it to produce a sunset effect, ranging from yellow through orange, pink, and purple to blue. Paint a narrow strip of yellow above the blue; this will appear behind the stars on the top border. If the paper wrinkles, iron it flat.

6 Carefully apply a thin layer of craft glue to the back of the

silhouette, omitting the bottom margin area. Place the painted paper on top, painted side down, and smooth it in place by running a wooden tongue depressor across the surface. Turn over the whole thing and carefully wipe away any excess glue that is visible on the other side.

7 Recut the slits at the top margin so that you cut through the painted paper. Fold the lantern along the score lines in the center of the trees

and glue the overlapping sides. Allow to dry.

8 Fold and interweave the top and bottom flaps inward along the margin score lines so that they are at right angles to the sides of the lantern, and glue into position. Allow to dry. Stick a tea light in a glass jar with a double-sided adhesive mounting pad (see p.10) and place it inside the lantern through the opening in the top.

Scallop Shells

Small jars containing tea lights are covered with colored tissue paper and sandwiched between pairs of scallop shells to create these unique lanterns. The elastic allows the jars to be inserted and removed easily, so make sure that the elastic is loose enough for you to insert a jar but tight enough to hold the shells in place. The jars need to fit snugly between the shells, so experiment with different shapes and sizes. Scallop shells can be obtained from specialist food stores or seafood restaurants.

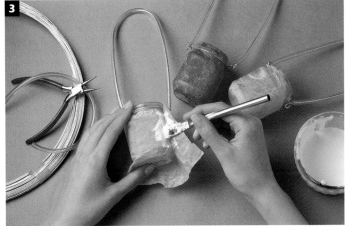

Materials (for each lantern)

- 2 evenly sized scallop shells
- Colored round elastic cord
- Galvanized wire
- Plastic tubing
- Small glass jar
- Paste (see p.14)
- Colored tissue paper
- Tea light
- Double-sided adhesive
  mounting pad

Equipment

- Drill
- Scissors
- Wire cutters
- Jewelry pliers
- Tape measure
- Brush and bowl for paste

1 Drill holes on both sides of the base of the shells and midway on each side.

2 Thread elastic through the base holes of two shells and tie together on the inside. Thread elastic through the holes on each side of the shells. Tie a knot at each end of both pieces of elastic on the insides of the shells.

3 Cut a length of wire and wrap it around the neck of the jar, using jewelry pliers to form two small loops on opposite sides of the jar (see p.12). Twist the ends of the wire together to secure in place. Cut 18in (45cm) of wire and 14in (35.5cm) of plastic tubing for the handle. Thread the wire through the tubing, with the excess wire protruding evenly. Push the excess wire through the loops on the jar, bend them upward with pliers, and squeeze tightly closed. Paste colored tissue paper around the jar.

4 Stick a tea light in the jar with a double-sided adhesive mounting pad. Open up the pair of shells and slip the jar inside.

Punched Tin Lantern

These delightful little lanterns are made from old beer cans and small drink cans. No special equipment is needed because the tin can be cut easily with all-purpose scissors and the pattern created by making holes with a pointed darning needle or with a paper punch. Once illuminated with a small flashlight or garden lights, the light will glow through the pierced patterns, creating a magical atmosphere for a mid-summer garden party. Always hang these lanterns safely away from where people are circulating as they can get very hot. Tea lights can be used to illuminate the cans, but candles do make these lanterns extremely hot and should be used with caution. Always wear protective gloves and goggles when you are working with tin and wire.

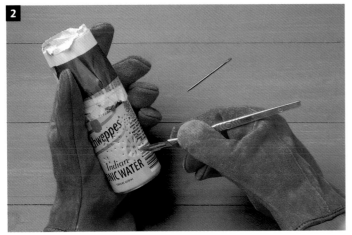

Materials

- Small soft drink can for main body of lamp
- Large soft drink can (for small lids) or beer can (for larger fluted edge lid)
- Newspaper
- Thin galvanized wire
- Small flashlight or string of garden lights

Equipment

- Fine-bladed craft knife
- Scissors or tin snips
- Wire cutter
- Pliers
- Pointed darning needle
- Felt tip pen
- Hole punch
- Template (see p.95)
- Cotter pins (split pins)

1 Use a craft knife to pierce a hole near the top rim of the small can large enough to insert tin snips or scissors. Cut around the rim to remove the top. Remove the top and bottom of the larger can. Keep the ring pulls.

2 Roll up a newspaper to fit inside the tin and make a design by piercing holes with a sharp implement, such as a craft knife or darning needle. If you wish, draw your pattern first with a felt tip pen.

3 Cut along the seam of the large can to open it up. Cut a pattern from the template and draw around it with a felt tip pen and cut out the shape.

4 Place the tin on a yielding surface (the back of a computer mouse mat or a telephone directory, for example) and pierce patterns with a darning needle or punch out larger holes with a paper hole punch.

5 Wrap the flat punched tin into a cone shape with an opening at the

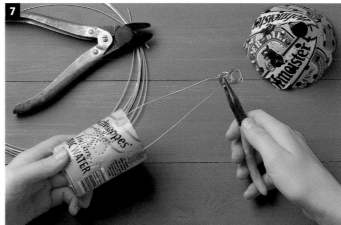

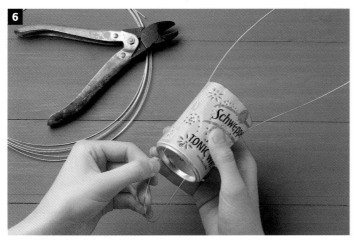

top and an overlap large enough to punch holes at the top and bottom. Secure it with cotter pins (split pins) through these holes.

6 Pierce two holes either side of the bottom of the small cans and two corresponding ones $\frac{1}{2}$in (1.25cm) down from the top rim. Cut a 20in (50cm) length of galvanized wire and thread either end in through the holes in the bottom of the can and out through the side holes.

7 Wrap the ends of the wire around the ring pull for hanging and secure with pliers.

8 Slide the lid over the wire hanger to fit on top of the can. You can bend the wires outward slightly to keep it in position. Place a small flashlight or a string of garden lights in the can. After the lantern has been used, remember to wait for the handle to cool down before touching it because it gets very hot.

Stars on Sticks

Lit by small flashlights, these portable stars could be carried in a procession or in a school Christmas play. You could also stick the cane into the ground or adapt the lantern so that it can be suspended from the branch of a tree. The paper used to cover the star has silk threads running through it, which make it more durable than ordinary tissue paper.

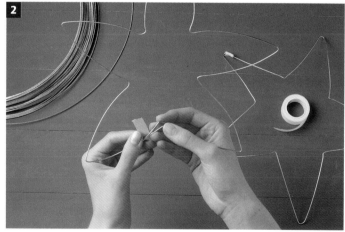

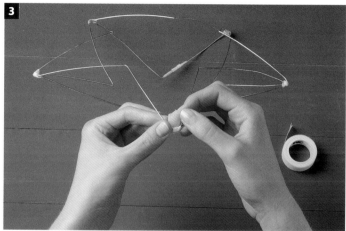

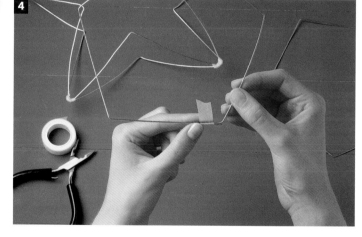

Materials (for each lantern)

- Galvanized wire
- Surgical tape
- Silk tissue paper
- Paste (see p.14)
- Bamboo stick
- Small camping flashlight

Equipment

- Wire cutters
- Tape measure
- Jewelry pliers
- Scissors
- Brush and bowl for paste

1 Cut two 45in (115cm) lengths of wire. Use pliers to bend the wire at 4in (10cm) intervals to form a zigzag shape (see p:12).

2 Bend each zigzag around to form a star and tape the overlapping wire to secure the shape in place.

3 Tape the two stars together at the tip of the points. Pull the center of each star outward to give the frame of a three-dimensional shape.

4 Cut two 21in (55cm) lengths of wire and use pliers to bend each one at 4in (10cm) intervals. Form each wire into a pentagon and tape the overlapping ends together to secure the shape.

5 Place a pentagon on one side of the star and tape the corners of the pentagon to the base of each pair of points of the star. Repeat with the second pentagon on the other side of the star.

6 Cut four 3½in (9cm) lengths of wire. Use pliers to form a hook at both ends of each wire (see p.12).

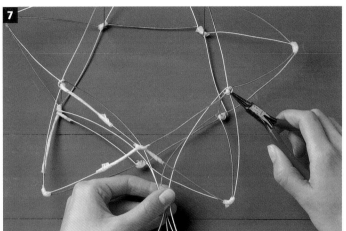

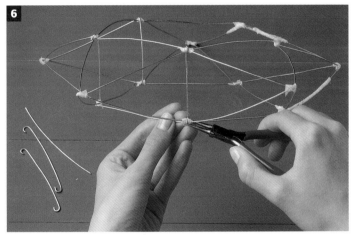

Fix the wires between the two pentagons by hooking them over the corners where the pentagons are taped to the star shapes. Squeeze the hooks closed using pliers. The corner without a wire will form the base of the star.

7 Cut four 10in (25cm) lengths of wire and form a hook at one end of each piece using pliers. Insert these through the base of the star, fastening one to each of the four corners of the pentagon on either side of the base of the star. Squeeze the hooks closed with pliers.

8 Cut out 10 triangular pieces of tissue paper to cover the points of the star, two pentagons to cover the center, and five diamonds to form the side pieces (see p.15). Cut each piece 1/2in (1.25cm) bigger all around than the shape it is to cover. Paste all the pieces into position on the front of the star and allow to dry. Repeat for the back of the star and then paste on the side pieces.

Snip the side piece that covers the base of the star into two triangles so that the wires can hang down. Let the lantern dry completely, then push the hanging wires into the center of a bamboo stick as far as they will go. You may need to trim them so that the cane meets the star. Tape a small flashlight onto the cane so that its head reaches up through the base and into the star.

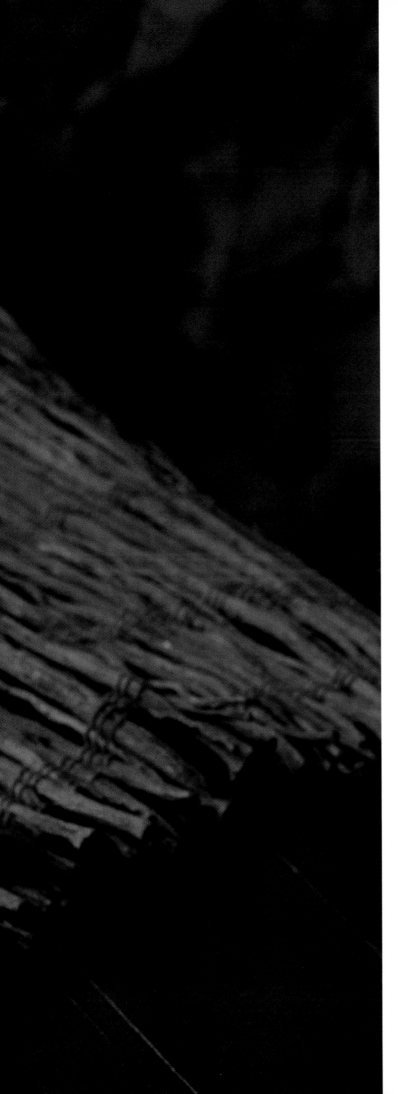

Teepee Table Light

Formed from a basic tripod structure, this table lamp is reminiscent of a teepee. Handmade silk tissue paper adorned with skeleton leaves covers the sides, while seedpods form the feet. A flap will let you insert a light. Make sure that the gap at the top of the lantern is directly over the flame to avoid hot spots. Skeleton leaves and seedpods are available from craft suppliers and florists.

Materials

- Willow sticks (withies)
- Raffia
- 3 hollow seedpods
- Strong glue
- White silk tissue paper
- Paste (see p.14)
- Colored tissue paper
- Skeleton leaves
- Tea light
- Lightweight glass container
- Double-sided adhesive
  mounting pad

Equipment

- Pruning shears
- Tape measure
- Glue applicator
- Scissors
- Brush and bowl for paste
- Craft knife

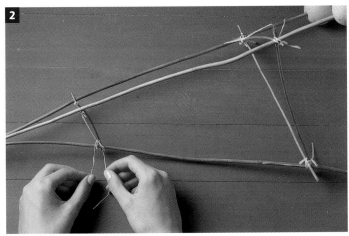

1 Cut three willow sticks (withies) 24in (61cm) long, three 10in (25cm) long, and three 4in (10cm) long. Tie the three long withies together at their thinner ends with raffia. Form the three shortest withies into a triangle and tie the ends together with raffia. Do the same with the three medium-sized ones. Insert the untied ends of the long willow sticks (withies) into the seedpods to make feet and secure with strong glue.

2 Insert the small triangle near the top of the tripod. Secure it in place at the corners with raffia. Do the same with the large triangle, securing it 3–4in (7.75–10cm) above the feet of the tripod.

3 Cut two pieces of silk tissue paper to fit the large triangle, allowing some overlap. Cut off the corners where the legs are. Paste both pieces into position, one on top and one underneath the triangle, wrapping the long edges around the triangle's framework (see p.15). Cut out pieces of silk paper for the sides of the tripod, to extend from the upper to the lower triangles. Paste them in place, wrapping the excess around the willow sticks (withies) where possible and overlapping it with the next side where it is not.

4 Once the paste has dried, mark the position of a doorway and cut it out using a craft knife (see p.15). Tear strips of colored tissue paper and paste them around the top and bottom edges of the teepee and around the doorway. Paste skeleton leaves onto the two uncut sides of the teepee. Stick a tea light in a lightweight glass container with a double-sided adhesive mounting pad (see p.10) and insert it through the doorway.

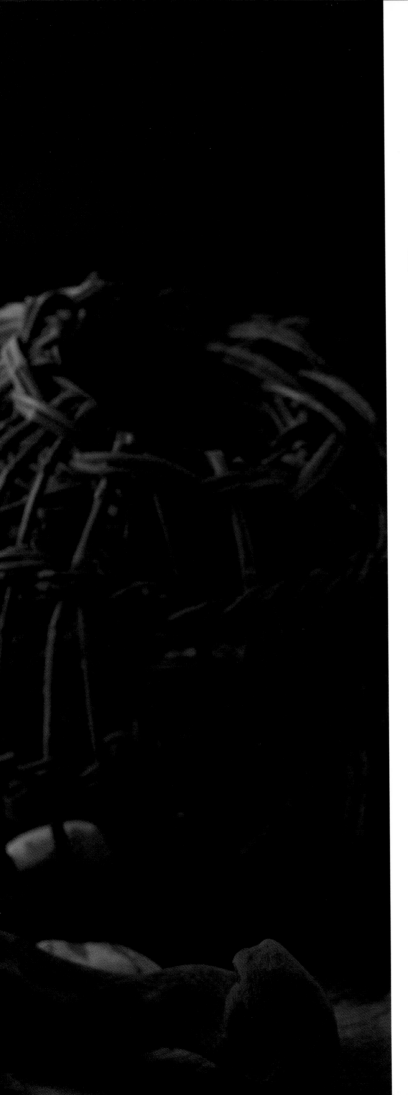

Marine Silhouette Lantern

This project is suitable for young children to make, as long as an adult does the cutting. Marine themes are always popular, and fish shapes are easy for children to draw. Alternatively, they could draw their own designs—a space scene with stars, planets, and rockets is another fun idea. This lantern is not designed to be carried, so make sure that you remove the light before picking it up.

Materials

- Thick dark blue cardstock
- Oil-resistant (greaseproof) baking paper
- Watercolor inks
- Craft glue
- Small round foil container
- Cotter pins (split-pins)
- Grommets (split-pin disks)
- Tea light
- Double-sided adhesive mounting pad

Equipment

- Fine-bladed craft knife or scissors
- Ruler, pencil, ballpoint pen
- Cutting board
- Paper for self-drawn stencil
- Sticky tack (Blu-Tack)
- Broad paintbrush
- Iron
- Brush and bowl for glue
- Wooden tongue depressor
- Cardboard tube
- Compass
- Eyelet punch

1 Cut a rectangle of blue cardstock measuring 15 x 10in (38 x 25cm) and draw a border 1in (2.5cm) in from the edge on all sides. Cut out the squares created where the lines intersect at each corner. Cut a rectangle of paper measuring 13 x 8in (33 x 20cm) and design your own marine stencil. Draw simple fish shapes and keep the shapes quite small. If you want to draw larger shapes, introduce stripes, as illustrated, so that the card holds

together with the backing paper when it is formed into a cylinder. Fix the stencil within the borders of the cardstock with removable adhesive mounting pads. Trace around the picture, pressing firmly, with a ballpoint pen.

2 Use a craft knife to cut out each shape in your marine scene.

3 Cut two 13 x 8in (33 x 20cm) rectangles of oil-resistant (greaseproof) baking paper. Use watercolor inks to paint one with

merging vertical stripes and the other with horizontal stripes. If the paper wrinkles, iron it flat once dry.

4 Stick one sheet on top of the other with a thin line of glue along their long edges; both painted sides should face in the same direction. Glue them to the blue cardstock, painted sides down, within the top and bottom margins. Fold over and glue these two margins to the back of the painted paper. Smooth the paper by running a wooden tongue depressor across it. Turn over the whole thing and carefully wipe away any excess glue that is visible on the other side.

5 Press the edge of a ruler firmly along the top and bottom borders so that they will curl, then roll the cardstock into a cylinder. Insert a cardboard tube to support the cylinder while you glue the overlapping edges together.

6 Use a compass and pencil to draw a 7¹⁄₂in (19cm) diameter circle on a piece of blue cardstock. Draw a 5¹⁄₂in (14cm) diameter circle centrally within it. Cut out the larger circle and snip from the edge to the inner circle at 1in (2.5cm) intervals. Bend these flaps up to form the base of the lantern.

7 Secure a foil container with a paper fastener to the center of the base circle of cardstock. Apply glue to the outside of the flaps, then insert the base into the cylinder and carefully press the flaps into place.

8 Cut a 16 x 1¹⁄₂in (40.5 x 4.75cm) strip of cardstock. Snip off the corners so that it has pointed ends. Use an eyelet punch to make a hole on opposite sides of the lantern ³⁄₄in (2cm) from the top and through each end of the handle. Position the handle so that the holes align with those in the lantern, and secure with cotter pins (split pins) and grommets (split-pin disks). Stick a tea light in the foil container with a double-sided adhesive mounting pad (see p.10).

63

Metallic Temple

This fabulous temple is ideal for special occasions, such as wedding anniversaries and christenings. It is constructed from an assortment of kitchen equipment, including empty food cans, baking pans, and graters, and held together with removable adhesive so that it stands securely but can be dismantled easily. A specific list of materials is given here, but you can improvise with whatever you have at hand.

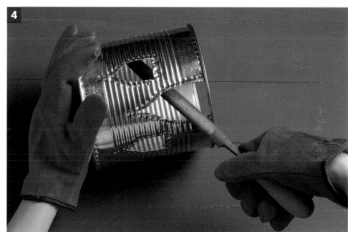

Materials

- 1 square cookie tin
- 1 extra-large round food can
- Sticky tack (Blu-Tack)
- 2 large round food cans
- 2 large, flat-backed, battery-operated lights
- Double-sided adhesive mounting pads
- 1 folding steamer
- 1 large and 2 small cheese graters
- 1 small bicycle light
- 3 brioche baking pans
- 1 small nutmeg grater
- 1 key-ring light
- Assortment of petit four baking pans
- 2 wire pan scourers
- 2 colanders
- Tea lights
- Small tin plates from a doll's house
- Shell-shaped madeleine baking pans

Equipment

- Paint stripper
- Steel wool
- Pencil or felt tip pen
- Square and round blocks of wood
- Vise (vice)
- Hammer
- Assortment of punches, nails, and chisels
- Metal file
- Protective gloves

1 If the cookie tin has a printed or painted finish remove it with paint stripper and steel wool. Draw a pattern on the tin with a pencil or felt tip pen. Put a square block of wood into a vise (vice) to hammer against, place one side of the tin over the wood, and, using an assortment of punches, nails, and chisels, hammer out your design.

2 Draw arabesque windows and doors on the largest food can. Place a round piece of wood in

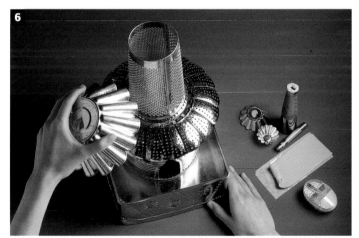

the vise (vice), hold the can in position with sticky tack (Blu-Tack), and hammer and chisel out the shapes. Decorate the can by punching patterns around it.

3 Repeat the process on the two remaining food cans.

4 Smooth any sharp edges around the doorways and windows with a metal file. Wear gloves to protect yourself from sharp, jagged edges.

5 Insert a large, flat-backed light into the base of the largest can and fix it in place with double-sided adhesive mounting pads. Do the same with the cookie tin. Invert the cookie tin and place the inverted large can on top of it.

6 Invert the folding steamer on top of the round can, then put a large cheese grater on top of this. Put a small bicycle light in the grater. Top this with an inverted brioche baking pan and then a nutmeg grater with a key-ring light inside. Finish the central tower with a petit four baking pan.

7 For each side tower, place an inverted brioche baking pan on top of a punched, round food can. Stretch a wire pan scourer around the base of a small cheese grater and place this on top of the tower. Add a turret of three petit four baking pans in diminishing sizes. To make the towers a little higher, stand each one on top of an inverted colander.

8 Once you have practiced putting the temple together, assemble it in the required location. Switch on each light and fix the sections together with sticky tack (Blu-Tack). To finish the scene, arrange tea lights on small tin plates and back them with shell-shaped madeleine baking pans to reflect the light.

Willow Fish Lantern

This handsome fish will illuminate your outdoor dining and inspire tall tales. Willow sticks (withies) are shaped to form the skeleton of the fish and then covered with tissue paper. Chicken wire is suspended inside to hold tea lights. To ensure that this fish does not get away, it is hung from fishing line and hooks. Use it on a dry, wind-free night and never leave it unattended while lit.

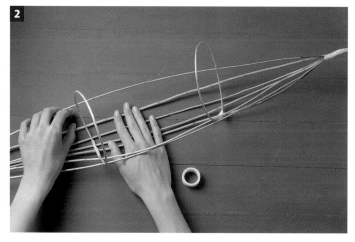

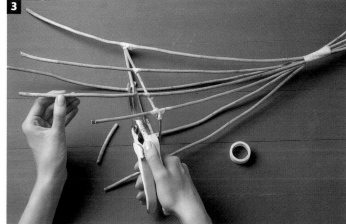

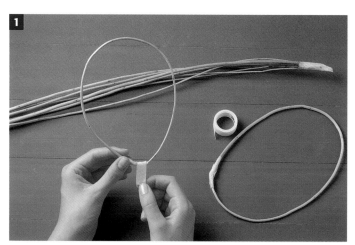

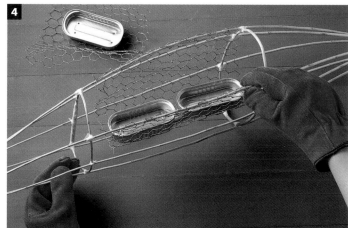

Materials

- Willow sticks (withies), soaked
- Surgical tape
- Chicken wire
- 3 small, shallow food cans
- Galvanized wire
- Plastic wrap (clingfilm)
- Paste (see p.14)
- Colored tissue paper
- Felt tip pens
- 3 tea lights
- 3 double-sided adhesive
  mounting pads

Equipment

- Pruning shears (secateurs)
- Tape measure
- Wire cutters
- Scissors
- Household pliers
- Brush and bowl for paste
- Craft knife

1 Cut seven 50in (130cm) long willow sticks (withies). Tape them together at their thinnest ends to make the nose of the fish. Tape them again 15in (38cm) from the other end to make the tail. Bend two more willow sticks (withies) into oval shapes, one measuring 7in (18cm) across its widest point and the other 6in (15cm), and fasten securely with tape (see p.12).

2 Slide the ovals inside the willow sticks (withies) that form the body of the fish, with the larger oval at the nose end and the smaller oval at the tail end. Spread the willow sticks (withies) around the ovals, making sure that there is one along the center bottom of the fish body and a 3in (8cm) gap between the two at the top of the body. Space the remaining willow sticks (withies) evenly and tape them to the ovals.

3 Bend a willow stick (withie) into a squat triangular shape and insert it between the willow sticks (withies)

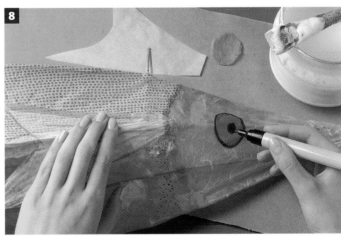

at the tail end of the fish. Position it so that the longest edge of the triangle runs from top to bottom of the fish. Tape it in place and trim the tail into an attractive shape.

4 Cut two pieces of chicken wire, one 11in (28cm) square and the other 11 x 6in (28 x 15cm). Pierce holes in the corners of three food cans using the points of a pair of scissors. Fasten two of the cans to the center of the large piece of chicken wire by cross-stitching through the holes and over

the chicken wire using galvanized wire. Twist the ends of the wire securely together using pliers. Bend the sides of the chicken wire upward to form an open basket, then lower it into the center of the fish. Wrap the top edges of the chicken wire basket around the top two willow sticks (withies). Fix the other can into the smaller piece of chicken wire and fasten it into the tail in a similar manner. Cover with plastic wrap, taking care to leave gaps

above the areas where the candles will be placed.

5 Paste blue tissue paper on top of the plastic wrap (see p.15) on the top half of the fish's body. Paste orange paper to the head, and red paper to the bottom half of the body and the tail.

6 When the fish is completely dry, start to decorate. Cut holes in the bottom half of the fish using a craft knife and paste circles of different colored paper over them (see p.15).

7 Paste pieces of blue tissue paper over parts of the tail. Add other colors along the edge of the tail.

8 Cut eyes and fins from tissue paper and paste them into position on either side of the fish. Once dry, use felt tip pens to add extra embellishment. Stick a tea light inside each of the food cans with double-sided adhesive mounting pads (see p.10) and suspend the fish from the tops of the two oval willow sticks (withies) within the fish body.

Flower Fairy Lantern

This flower fairy holds a pretty bluebell lantern to light her way. The lantern is a bluebell, but you could adapt the colors to create other hanging blossoms if you wish. The fairy's wings are made from nylon panty hose stretched over a wire framework with glitter glued around the edges to add strength and sparkle. The wings are attached with elastic arm straps which can be hidden with a feather trim.

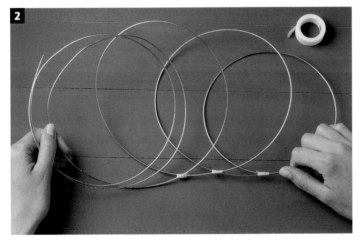

Materials

■ Galvanized wire

■ Surgical tape

■ Tissue paper

■ Paste (see p.14)

■ Watercolor ink

■ Green gardening wire

■ Bamboo stick

■ Glass jar

■ Tea light or bicycle light

■ Double-sided adhesive pad

■ Cup hook

■ Strong glue

Equipment

■ Wire cutters

■ Tape measure

■ 4–5in (10–12.75cm) diameter
cylinder, such as a pipe or
large can

■ Small bowl

■ Scissors

■ Brush and bowl for paste

■ Medium paintbrush

■ Jewelry pliers

■ Glue applicator

1 Cut a 10ft (3m) length of galvanized wire and bend it around a cylinder to form six complete loops (see p.12).

2 Remove the wire from the cylinder and spread out the loops so that they lie side by side. Tape the crossover point at the base of each loop to secure it in place.

3 Bend the loops around to form a flower shape and tape the overlapping ends together to hold the structure in place.

4 Gently squeeze the sides of each petal to form points at the end. Tape the sides of the petals together so that they are held side by side but do not overlap. Draw around one of them to make a petal template.

5 Place a small bowl in the center of the petals and bend them up around it to form a bell-shaped flower.

6 Use the petal template to cut out six pieces each of blue and pink tissue paper, allowing a 1in (2.5cm) overlap all the way around (see p.15). Paste the blue tissue paper to the outside of the wire flower's petals, wrapping the edges around the wire and trying to keep the paper as smooth as possible.

Make sure that the central base of the flower is not covered.

7 Paste the pink tissue paper to the inside of each petal. Allow to dry.

8 When completely dry, curl the tips of the petals outward slightly. Paint outlines and detail on the petals with watercolor ink. Tissue paper colors fade quickly, so store the flower away from direct sunlight.

9 To make leaves, cut 6ft (180cm) of galvanized wire and bend it back on itself about 15in (38cm) from

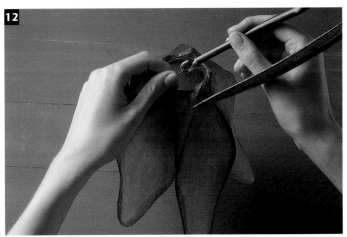

each end. Use pliers to loop the ends around the main wire (see p.12), then bend the whole thing just below one of the leaves. Spread out the bent-back wire to form two leaf shapes and cover with green tissue paper in the same way as the petals.

10 Use green gardening wire to bind the leaves securely to a bamboo stick.

11 Cover a glass jar with white tissue paper and decorate it with ink. Cut a length of galvanized wire and wrap it around the neck of the jar, using jewelry pliers to form two small loops on opposite sides of the jar (see p.12). Twist the ends of the wire around each other tightly to secure the wire in place. Bend a short length of galvanized wire into a handle, push the ends down through the loops on the jar, then bend them upward with pliers. Squeeze these hooks tightly closed to secure the handle to the jar. Stick a tea light or a small reflective bicycle light in the jar with a double-sided adhesive mounting pad (see p.10).

12 Screw a cup hook into the top of the bamboo stick and secure with strong glue if necessary. Place the flower over the glass jar so that the handle emerges through the base of the flower. Reshape the handle if necessary so that it supports the flower. Loop the handle over the hook on the end of the cane.

Geometric Glow-light

A 12-sided paper globe with the top facet missing makes a perfect lantern. The tea light inside illuminates the hand-painted watercolor paper to reveal the stars formed by the overlapping glued edges. If you wish, you could use inks or felt tip pens to accentuate the stars for a more dramatic effect, or make the globe from plain white paper for a minimalist look.

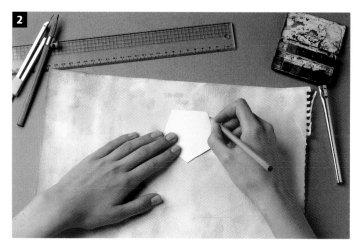

Materials

- Sheet of watercolor paper at least 12 x 17in (30 x 43cm)
- Watercolor paints
- Craft glue
- Cooking oil
- Tea light
- Lightweight glass container
- Double-sided adhesive mounting pad

Equipment

- Masking tape
- Broad and medium paintbrushes
- Photocopy of template (see p.94)
- Pencil
- Scissors
- Compass
- Ruler
- Brush and bowl for glue
- Brush and bowl for oil
- Wooden tongue depressor or similar implement
- Paper towels

1 Tape the paper onto a flat surface and use a large brush to wet it with water. The tape will hold the wet paper in place and stop it from wrinkling. Dip a medium brush into some paint, then touch the tip of the brush to the paper. The color will flow out across the wet paper. Repeat this process with different colors all over the paper, allowing them to blend together. Let it dry.

2 Place the photocopied template on the colored paper and draw around it with a pencil. Draw 11 pentagons in total.

3 Cut out the pentagons and mark the midpoint on each of the five sides. Score lines from the midpoint of one side to the midpoint of the adjacent side, using a ruler and the point of a compass. Take care not to press too deeply so that you do not cut through the paper.

4 Choose one pentagon as the base. Attach a pentagon to each side of the base pentagon, gluing

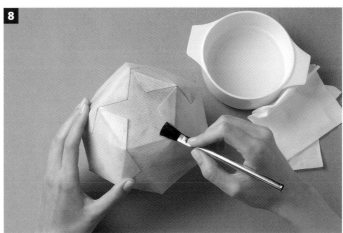

along one of the scored flaps. Run a wooden tongue depressor across the glued flaps to spread the glue, then wipe away any excess. The finished piece should form a star shape.

5 Bend the surrounding pentagons up to form a bowl shape, gluing together the overlapping flaps.

6 Glue the remaining five pentagons onto the bowl structure to form the top part of the lantern. Each new piece should be over-lapped on four sides by the flaps of four different pentagons. Although it does not matter whether each piece overlaps on the inside or the outside—the star shape will still show when the lantern is lit—it is best to have a consistent pattern.

7 Fold over and glue the remaining flaps onto the inside of the globe, leaving a pentagonal hole.

8 Warm some cooking oil and brush this all over the outside of the lantern. Allow it to soak into the paper for a minute or two, then wipe off the excess with paper towels. This will make the lantern more translucent. Stick a tea light in a lightweight glass container with a double-sided adhesive mounting pad (see p.10) and place it inside the lantern.

String of Lights

A plain string of christmas lights has been transformed by colorful lanterns into the perfect party illuminations. Each droplet is made from wire covered with tissue paper. They are not waterproof, so beware of sudden downpours. To make a shimmering centerpiece for a room, an individual lantern could be scaled up to make a table lamp, but make sure that you use a low-wattage bulb.

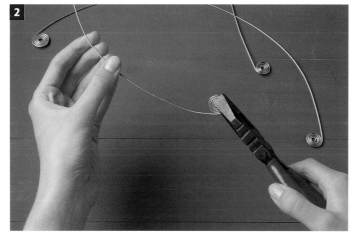

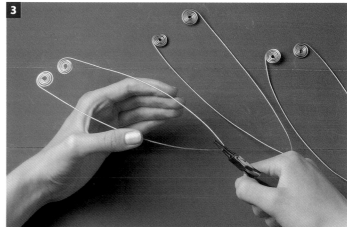

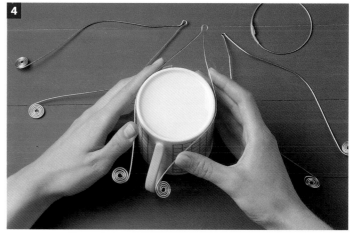

Materials

- Galvanized wire
- Surgical tape
- Green gardening wire
- Colored tissue paper
- Paste (see p.14)
- String of outdoor christmas lights

Equipment

- Wire cutters
- Tape measure
- Jewelry pliers
- Household pliers
- Cup
- 2in (5cm) diameter cylinder
- Scissors
- Brush and bowl for paste

1 For each arabesque-shaped lantern, cut three 26in (70cm) lengths of galvanized wire. Form a loop at each end of each wire using jewelry pliers (see p.12).

2 Use household pliers to wind the loops into a flat spiral (see p.12), each about ½in (1cm) in diameter.

3 Hold one of the pieces of wire at its center point with jewelry pliers and push the ends of the wire together to form a looped angle (see p.12). Repeat with the

remaining two wires. To vary the shape of the lanterns, bend some so that the spirals curl inward and some so that they curl outward.

4 Wrap each piece of wire around the base of a cup and bend the wire so that it forms an elegant arabesque arch shape.

5 Tape the sharply bent areas of the three pieces of wire together, spreading out the wires to form six evenly spaced struts. Form a circle of galvanized wire around a 2in

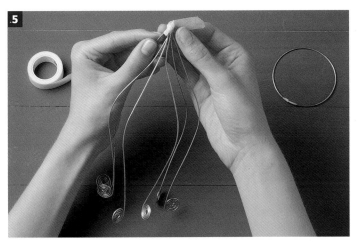

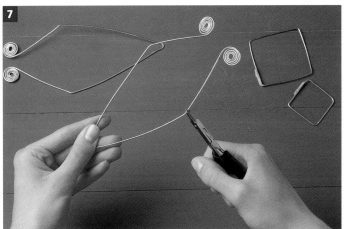

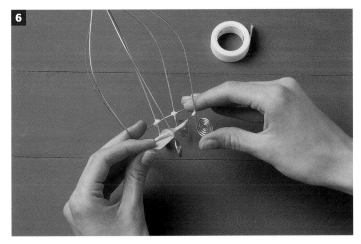

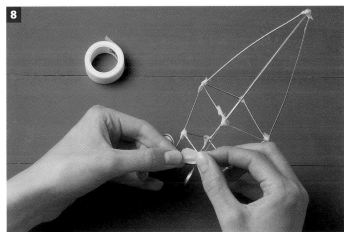

(5cm) diameter cylinder, taping the overlapping ends together (see p.12).

6 Insert the circle between the six struts, just above the spirals, and tape it in position, making sure that the space between each strut is even.

7 To make a diamond-shaped lantern, follow steps 1, 2, and 3 but using only two pieces of wire. Bend an angle slightly above the halfway mark on each wire strut

using jewelry pliers. Bend two lengths of galvanized wire into squares, one 1 1/2in (4cm) and the other 2in (5cm). Tape the overlapping ends together.

8 Insert the large square between the four struts and tape it at each corner to the bent angles of the struts. Tape the smaller square just above the spirals.

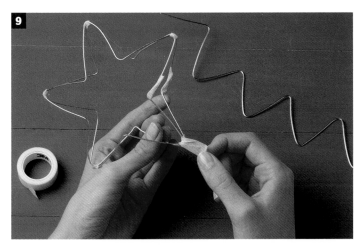

9 Cut two 22in (56cm) lengths of galvanized wire for each star lantern. Bend each one into a zigzag at 2in (5cm) intervals, making five points plus a little wire left at the end to form an overlap (see p.12). Bend the wire around to form a star and tape the overlapping ends together.

10 Tape the two stars together at the tips of the points, then pull the center of each star outward to give the frame a fuller shape. Cut two

7in (18cm) lengths of gardening wire and bend each piece in half. Push the looped corner up through the base of the star at the inner angle of a pair of points, then push the two ends of the wire through the loop and pull downward, as shown. Repeat on the opposite side of the star with the other wire. Cut pieces of tissue paper to cover all the facets of the star except the base where the wires emerge and paste in place (see p.15).

11 Paste tissue paper over the arabesque- and diamond-shaped lanterns in the same way, using a variety of patterns and colors (see p.15). Make sure that you leave the area between the spirals uncovered so that you can insert lights.

12 Insert lengths of gardening wire through each of the spirals of the arabesque- and diamond-shaped lanterns. When all of the lanterns are finished, insert a mini-light from the string of christmas lights into

each one and secure the lantern in place by twisting the gardening wire around the main cable of the christmas lights. Take care that the bulbs do not touch the tissue paper (see p.11).

Crescent Moon

A large structure such as this looks fantastic in a procession. For safety reasons, it should be worn only by a healthy adult who has no back problems in dry, wind-free conditions. If it is going to be worn for a prolonged period, foam padding can be taped to the backpack at any points where the support is likely to rub. It is easiest to work in pairs when building a backpack. Alternatively, you could make the moon lantern without the frame to carry it (starting from step 5) and suspend it from a high ceiling or tree branch for a eye-catching centerpiece.

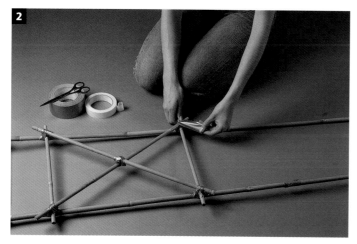

Materials

- Bamboo canes of even thickness
- Masking and heavy-duty tape
- Nylon webbing for straps
- 2 bathroom sponges
- 22 soaked willow sticks (withies) 7ft (110cm)
- 3 lightweight flashlights
- Green gardening wire
- Plastic wrap (clingfilm)
- Paste (see p.14)
- White and yellow tissue paper
- 6 self-adhesive Velcro pads

Equipment

- Tape measure
- Saw
- Scissors
- Pruning shears
- Wire cutters
- Brush and bowl for paste
- Craft knife

1 Measure the person who is to carry the lantern: shoulder width, hip width, from hip to shoulder, from hip to top of head, from hip to base of buttock, and diagonal from outside of hip to opposite shoulder. Add 2in (5cm) to each measurement. Saw two bamboo canes 4ft (125cm) longer than the hip to head measurement and lay them on the floor parallel to each other. Add the hip width and shoulder width measurements together and divide in half. Cut three bamboo canes this length. Put one of the canes underneath the uprights at one end. This marks the base of the buttocks. Place a cane on top of the two uprights at the hip and shoulder points. Cut two canes to reach diagonally from hips to opposite shoulders and lay these in place. Allow 1in (2.5cm) of stick to protrude at all the intersections.

2 Tape all the joints together with masking tape, then double-check

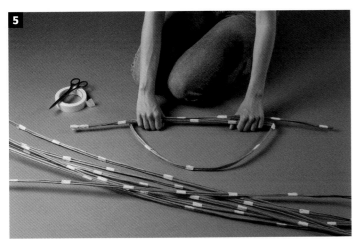

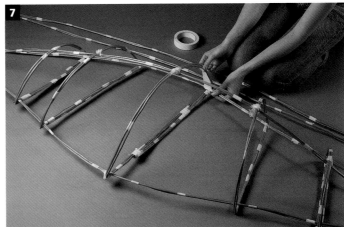

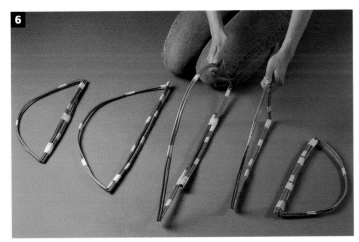

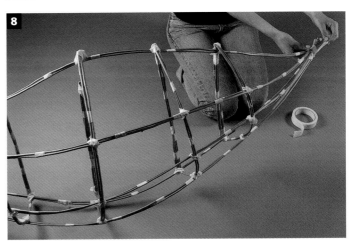

the measurements. Make any necessary adjustments, then tape the joints tightly with heavy-duty tape, criss-crossing it around the sticks (see p.13).

3 Cut two lengths of webbing, each equal to the height of the person who is to carry the lantern, and tie each one securely to a shoulder joint on the frame. Tape over this knot with heavy-duty tape. Place the frame against the back of the person.

4 Cross the lengths of webbing over the chest, inserting a sponge under each one at the shoulders to prevent the webbing from digging in, then bring the tapes around and under the hip bar and tie securely. Secure the sponges in place with heavy-duty tape, then remove the structure.

5 To make the moon, tape willow sticks (withies) together, thin end to thick end, to make eleven pairs (see p.13). Bend one pair into a D shape (see p.13), so that the ends on the

flat side overlap. Tape along the overlapping side and trim off any excess. The D should measure about 13in (33cm) deep and 20in (51cm) along the flat side.

6 Make four more D shapes in the same way, the first two 14in (35.5cm) long and 9in (23cm) deep, and the second two 12in (30.5cm) long and 7in (17.75cm) deep. Lay them out on the floor so that the largest is in the middle and the smallest ones are at either end.

7 Insert two pairs of willow sticks (withies) through the D shapes, positioning one pair at each row of corners. Tape the largest D shape to the two pairs of willow sticks (withies), making sure that the D shape is at the center of their length. Insert a third pair of willow sticks (withies) through the D shapes and tape it to the center of the curves at evenly spaced intervals.

8 Bend the structure into a crescent moon, with the curve of the

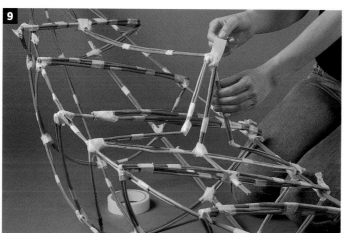

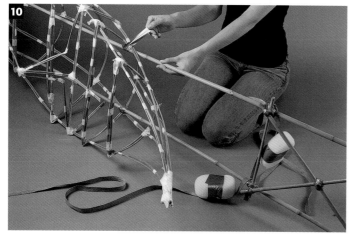

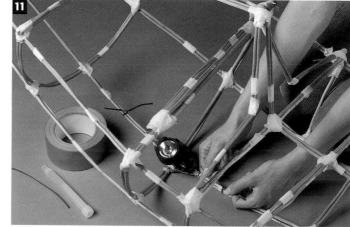

D shapes forming the back of the moon. Tape the ends of the long willow sticks (withies) together into points and then tape them to the remaining corners of the D shapes. Tape two more pairs of willow sticks (withies) along the length of the moon on the outside of the D shapes, positioned halfway between the willow sticks (withies) on the central curve and those at the corners.

9 To make the nose, hold the moon shape with its straight side facing you. Tape the last pair of willow sticks (withies) to one of the corner struts on the inside of the small D shape at the top of the moon. Bend it outward, then bend it sharply back into the moon halfway between the central and second lowest D shapes. Allow it to point out about 8in (20cm) at its tip. Bend the remaining end sharply downward to rest on the second lowest D shape. Use the offcuts of willow sticks (withies) to form the base of the nose, stretching them across the flat side of the moon between the central and second lowest D shapes, and bending them out to the tip of the nose. It is important that the nose has an adequate framework for attaching tissue paper (see p.15).

10 Slide the protruding bamboo canes at the top of the backpack into the moon between the side struts that lie on the curves of the D shapes. Insert the bamboo through the curve of the second lowest D and up through to the front of the top D. The back of the backpack should be in the same direction as the moon's face. Tape the bamboo at all points of contact with heavy-duty tape and shake the structure firmly to check that it is secure.

11 Attach the flashlights to the structure, one fastened to the center back so that the beam points toward the nose, and the other two pointing to the center

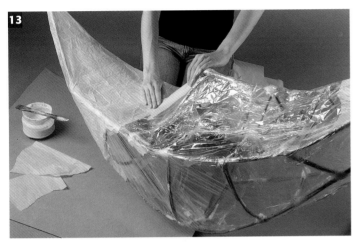

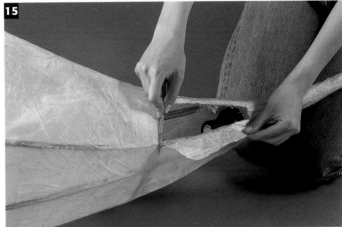

of the moon from the top and bottom tips. Use gardening wire to position them, then tape them securely in place with heavy-duty tape, avoiding the battery and bulb access points.

12 Cover the whole structure with plastic wrap (see p.14). Paste large pieces of white tissue paper randomly all over the moon to help diffuse the light (see p.15).

13 When dry, cover the white paper with a layer of yellow paper. You may need more than one layer, depending on the type of tissue you use.

14 Cut out eyes and a mouth from yellow tissue paper and paste them onto the moon. When dry, use a marker pen to draw in detail. Allow to dry.

15 Using a craft knife, cut flaps through the tissue in front of the top and bottom flashlights and at the side of the back flashlight (see p.15). Make them large enough to allow access to the flashlights in order to turn them on and off and to replace batteries.

16 Paste a ½in (1cm) border of tissue around the cut edges of the flaps so that they overlap the opening. Allow to dry, then stick Velcro pads to the top and bottom of each flap so that they can be opened and closed.

Templates

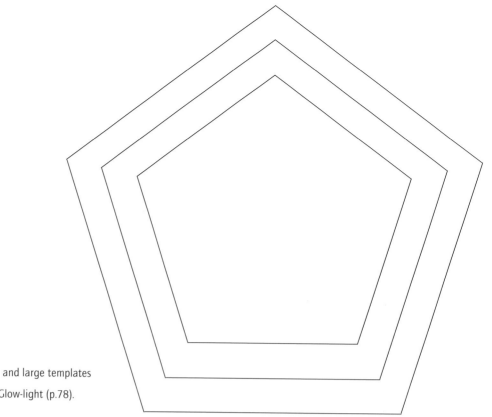

Small, medium and large templates
for Geometric Glow-light (p.78).

Template for Punched Tin Lantern (p.48).

Template for
Goblin Night Light (p.40).
(You will need to
enlarge this template
by 150 per cent.)

Index

Resources

Wire, pliers and other materials used in this book are readily available at most hardware, home improvement and art and craft retailers. Below is home office information for finding the store closest to you, and some specialty suppliers that you can contact for mail order service.

THE BUILDING BOX
In Canada: (877) 277-3651
www.thebuildingbox.com
HOME DEPOT (US AND CAN)
In the US: (770) 433-8211

In Canada: (800) 668-226
www.homedepot.com
LOWE'S HOME IMPROVEMENT WAREHOUSE
In the US: (800) 44-LOWES
www.lowes.com
MACPHERSON CRAFT SUPPLIES
In Canada: (519) 284-1741
www.macphersoncrafts.com
MENARDS
In the US: (612) 946-5380
MICHAELS STORES, INC.
In the US: (800) MICHAELS
www.michaels.com

PARAMOUNT WIRE CO.
In the US: (973) 672-0500
www.parawire.com
PAUL GESSWEIN & CO INC
In the US: (800) 243-4466
In Canada: (800) 263-6106
www.gesswein.com
REVY HOME & GARDEN WAREHOUSES AND HOME CENTERS
In western Canada: (604) 882-6200
In eastern Canada: (416) 241-8844
www.revy.com
WIRE MART INTERNATIONAL
In the US: (800) 829-8936

With thanks to:

Andy Boal for the Crescent Moon; Floris Books for the Geometric Glow-light design from Christmas Crafts by Thomas Berger; Penny Bowlan who gave me the Metallic Temple idea; and Mick Clark for allowing us to use his garden. Thanks also to my three patient models, Bryony Maguire-Gillmore, Dominic Walker, and Ruben Johnson; to Peter Williams for producing wonderful photographs in challenging circumstances and; Georgina Rhodes for her magical styling and book design.